MW00937211

Chalk Dustings

by Gloria MacKay

Gloria MacKay

Original title
Chalk Dustings

Cover design
Sonja Smolec

Layout & graphics
Sonja Smolec, Yossi Faybish

Published by
Aquillrelle

ISBN 978-1-105-62103-1

MacKay 3677

Table of Contents

Chalk Dustings

Foreword: *A Soft Place to Fall*

I don't always do well with poetry. My own? The writing remains a mystery, yet unsolved. Other people's? Some rhyme, some don't, some try. Some march in lock step while others sashay all over the page, and anything measured in iambs is too uptown for me. And yet...?

I spent half my life—not my first years nor recent years but the rest—stumbling over poetry: A reflex, perhaps, such as ducking in a tunnel or always facing the door when you're in an elevator. A futile pursuit, for sure, for a word lover like me, back-pedaling whenever a bit of poetry pops up, as harmless as one of those roly poly clowns babies love to bat around.

In this middle stretch of my life, if I had been called upon to recite, the only lines of poetry I knew were snippets I learned in the fourth grade: they were in my face all day long. I loved them. Still do.

Our classroom had a cloak closet (no, I don't go back far enough for cloaks but apparently the closet did) that extended across front of the room behind the teacher's desk. At the sound of the morning bell four door monitors (changed weekly) lowered the four sliding doors, raised them before lunch, lowered them after lunch, and raised them again at the end of the day.

These barriers stifled smells of galoshes and wet wool and lessened the scent of tuna fish sandwiches warming up. The odor of over-ripening bananas, however, oozed through the cracks undeterred. Whenever I encounter a brown banana the shades of my memory rise and my fourth grade classroom appears, closet doors going up, lunch about to begin.

The fronts were faced with rectangles of cork so riddled with thumbtack holes they looked like targets and squares of blackboard, usually smudged with chalk dust but occasionally streaky clean.

If the smelly closet was the sow's ear, Miss Gallagher's poems had to be the silk purse. Every Monday morning we came upon her, virgin stick of chalk in hand, writing the Poem of the Week on the blackboard; her penmanship was protractor perfect. Every morning, after the flag salute, we read the poem together out loud. Every afternoon we wrote it on special handwriting paper. On Friday we were expected to recite every word from memory.

I have not forgotten the first four lines of the first poem of fourth grade inscribed on the cloak closet door:

I saw you toss the kites on high
And blow the birds about the sky.
And all about I heard you pass
Like ladies' skirts across the grass.

This is the best poem in the world, trembled my fourth grade heart, failing to grasp this was the first poem entering my nine year old heart. Robert Louis Stevenson gave me a vision: one day I, too, would rustle across the grass, a lady at last. I did not foresee I would love growing up to be a woman but not always want to be a lady. It was enough that the words made me happy.

As autumn wore on, fog appeared on little cat feet, sat on silent haunches looking over harbor and city and then moved on, either up or down according to the time of the day. I gripped my sturdy pencil and tried to make my handwriting as flawless as Carl Sandburg's imagination.

One Monday morning in spring we read together:

I think that I shall never see
A poem lovely as a tree.
A tree whose hungry mouth is pressed
Against the earth's sweet loving breast.
Upon whose bosom snow has lain
Who intimately lives with rain.

The strain of comparing a poem to a tree or turning a breast into a figure of speech was nothing compared to the stir Miss Gallagher caused when she told us Joyce Kilmer was a man. The class could tell she didn't want a lot of questions why this was, so we snickered behind our hands.

After the fourth grade, poetry was no longer a part of my life. I don't know why, it just wasn't; I didn't look for it and it didn't look for me. Not until the musty books of high school did I again come nose to nose with a poem: Edgar Alan Poe with his tintinnabulating bells and that pesky talking bird; John Donne's "no man is an island" and Henry Wadsworth Longfellow's decision to make "children's hour" rhyme with "night that is beginning to lower". Not that there is anything wrong with that, but I yearned for those happy words from Miss Gallagher. When in doubt, regress, I guess.

Next, I leaped into novels: Thomas Wolfe said you can't go home, again so I didn't. Still no more poetry for me ... until college, where the poems I stumbled through were nothing like the life I was stumbling through. What I was ready for but did not know it (how can one find what they don't know exists?) was a lower case e and e cummins and Eliot with a capital T. S. Instead, I struggled with ... *Gather ye rosebuds while you may ... When I was one and twenty ... And oh, 'tis true, 'tis true.* Not that there is anything wrong Herrick and Houseman, I figured out later, but I was so not there at the time.

Not since the fourth grade had poetry and I been at the same place at the same time in the same frame of mind. Insomnia and an old *Atlantic Monthly* intervened. I woke up, got up, stumbled around for something to read, dug to the bottom of the basket in the corner by the couch and came up with a magazine, folded to an unread page. I knew it was unread because I had tossed into the basket months before. The sidebar said this feature includes a poem inside a short story embedded in a novel by Cynthia Ozick: *The Puttermesser Papers*.

A bit too contrived for my taste. But it was 2 am and I was wide-eyed. READ IT thumped my fourth grade heart. I did until my lids dropped and the only words between me and THE END was the poem. It clawed at me. I was too tired to resist.

At the point of a knife
I lost my life.

Butter, butter, butter
butter knife.

If I were alive I wouldn't fault
anything under the heavenly vault.

Better, better, better
better life.

Better never to have loved than loved at all.
Better never to have risen than had a fall.

Oh, bitter, bitter, bitter
butter
knife.

This is the best poem I ever read, trembled my weary, forgetful heart as I turned out the lights. Wind wiggled the blinds; fog crept in; trees nodded as I stumbled into bed. I curled up with poetry; it was a soft place to fall.

Chalk Dustings

Eye Openers

I have never met the woman who hangs hooks
on the outsides of her doors
where everyone can see them.
Not hangs, actually, screws.
She screws hooks into the outsides of her doors and closets,
into plasterboard and cove moldings
and on either side of the gold-framed mirror in the hallway
where one is likely to pause
for a place to hang a purse or shawl
or pantyhose or anything extraneous at the moment.
She also sews her own aprons,
with pockets large enough for extra hooks, and cookies
for children who knock just to ask,
"Why do you have a hook right under the doorbell?"

She also paints, so says her son The Artist
who boasts she inherited her talent from him,
not with rollers to freshen the walls,
they have to be spackled first.
His mother paints still life.
Still lifes or still lives?
Whatever, she has lots, neatly framed,
hanging on nails among the hooks,
price tags dangling.
I would buy one if I knew where she lived.
Which one, I wonder?
I am not fond of bananas.
That's one thing I like about children.
They knock and eat cookies.
They're not choosy.

With Lilac Trees

I feel disconnected living so high off the ground
as though I have misplaced something,
like the baby.

I find myself hurrying from the mailbox
listening for the baby.
Throwing my arm across the car seat when I stop

groping for the baby.
Sorting laundry hit-or-miss, not my usual style,
where is the baby's pile,

where's his blankie, where's his smile?
There was a baby once,
several, to be exact

in the playpen on the grass.
Not a bunch, like rosy radishes
but one by one, as babies come,

and one by one, they go. I know.
With lilac trees and shoes with cleats
packed with memories and last year's seeds.

My mailbox has a number I can't begin to see
from three storeys in the air
where I hang fuchsias on the deck

and watch the sun drop through the trees
and sniff, as fragrances drift past
like babies footprints in the grass.

Reader's Lament

Words await me
out there in the dark,
on the table by the couch
next to my glasses.
My new skinny navy blue wires
and those oversized gold ones for older readers,
bifocals precisely incised. I can read with either.

In the morning I always find them together
where the books are
as though there's been a party
and I wasn't invited.
I don't like to turn off the lights
and go to bed, leaving unseen words behind
like children I have never met
or chocolates in the box,

but even readers need to sleep.
So there I lie with twitching legs
and sweaty head not meant to dent a pillow
reusing worn out dreams
like threadbare jeans
while down the hallway pages wave
as words creep out in conga lines
slithering through the night.

And Then There Were Four

I collect words … a worthwhile hobby for a woman like me, one with neither room nor inclination for stuff (brooches, antiques, silver spoons and the like) and a reluctance to hang my passions on the wall.

My computer greets me with a new word each day. Occasionally I throw one in the trash as I would a cracked tea cup or musty paperback, but most words pile on my hard drive like fallen leaves. When I fear they will clog my machine I burn them into a CD and set them aside.

I like words best when they string together like beads; they are easier to remember this way. Snippets from stand-up comic Stephen Wright, for instance, swipe through my mind like a credit card:

> *What's another word for Thesaurus?*
> *On the other hand you have different fingers.*

or an aside from Woody Allen: *I am not afraid of death. I just don't want to be there when it happens.* I chuckle every time.

I tend to mark different chapters in my life with pithy little thoughts I come upon, turning them over in my mind so often they become, I must admit, trite. This is what I collect, personal clichés, repeated reminders that I did the best I could with what I knew at the time.

My collection is smaller than most. For years there were three. The first has a Shakespearean ring, perhaps a Biblical tone. I can almost hear the phrase in the mutterings of Hamlet, except these must be the words of a woman.

What is hard to endure is sweet to recall.

I scoffed when I first heard this, but it remained in my head as patiently as a book waiting to be read. As I was growing up and growing old there were times when I could scarcely endure my family ... the year I cooked my first turkey and my dad insisted he stick his camera batteries in my oven to "charge them up a bit"; the Christmas he had that same frayed accordion pleated camera turned backwards and took a flash of his nose and my mother laughed so hard she fell over and flattened the tree. The baby started chewing on tinsel. I never would have believed it, but these are sweet memories to me now.

As years passed another keeper doubled my collection.

The best revenge is a good life.

This advice so heartened me I shared it with my children in the guise of motherly wisdom. "What is a good life, anyway." snorted one son, in the throes of adolescent pain.

"You'll know it when you see it," I replied. The moment I spoke I knew I sounded smug, but what is a mother to say when she wants to help but she can't? She does her best or she does nothing.

Years passed until I added a third: it is a statement of fact – as terse and pragmatic as any dead-pan delivery by a comedian ... except it isn't funny. The French think *c'est la vie,* Sinatra croons *that's life.* What I learned to say to anyone who would listen was...

Loving your bargain doesn't make it painless to pay the bill.

20

I knew this, but I didn't know that I knew until I found these words, like a prize in a box of Cracker Jack, in *Sabbatical*, a novel by John Barth. No hint of angry little ego or mawkish retrospection here. A statement of fact, tucked in my brain like a roll of tightly wrapped coins.

I intended these three bits of wisdom to see me through to the end. But there is one good thing about being a collector of words, there is always room for one more, as we lovers of the cliché utter at the drop of a hat.

I came upon a fresh string of words as inadvertently as plucking a four-leafed clover in the grass. It is almost too bumper sticker cute, except it has a piquancy about it, an irony, appealing, perhaps, to someone my age.

Wherever you go there you are.

Just thinking it makes me smile, but I'm apt to say it out loud when I can't think of anything else to say. Children, in particular, often respond with a quick but gentle nod of understanding.

It's a Wrap

I can coax a roll of skinny ribbon into sausage curls
with my thumb and an old pair of shears,
to say nothing
of hustling
glitzy sheets of gift wrap
snapping like taffeta
down and around corners
as crisply as bed sheets
in some fancy dancy hotel,
and while I'm at it
stack scads of never been stuck on
stick-on bows in ziplocked bags ... pre-sorted by color.

I love brown paper bags
white walls
tawny teak tables,
my little black dress, and pearls,
two, one in each ear.
I love stainless steel sinks,
faded navy sweats,
cars without a lot of chrome
and absolutely no gold trim
and my everyday friends,
who, too, wrap with pizzazz
but remain plain.
No razzamatazz.

The All Grin No Sin Blues

Sometimes a different god speaks to me in sounds I only feel.
Not the god on nickels in whom we trust
nor the one on our side, watching football Sunday afternoons,
no scratch match there. Might as well nap.

Not the god of everlasting life sweet-talking my soul,
nor some whodoo voodoo, jabberwocking up and down my spine
like magic. Another one. A happy days are here again
the skies above are clear again god, leaving traces of a

smiley face never quite erased from my cut and pasted brain.
Not immutable, I guess, like all the rest, unless eternity
has never really been a where or when affair. Every time I press
a shell against my ear, eternity is now, or feel a Mona

Lisa smile smudged against my cheek or glance up and spot
a quirky cat afloat among the clouds (all grin, no sin)
I feel a different god, strumming, almost humming, the emanating,
transubstantiating, let us sing a song of cheer again blues.

As They Say

I live in a soft-sculptured world,
standing tall, as they say,
in a bean bag chair sort of way.
Corners not mitered, no matter, bed's made.
Hair uncombed ... but with a good cut.

I'm no crazy quilt, hand-stitched around polkas and dots
upside down in the mirror.
I have structure, as they say,
my posts and beams well-anchored in a topsy turvy way
like a Dali clock sprawled across time

ticking fine.
Nor am I some basted body bag of crepy skin,
chalking days with a squeak,
marking time as they say
in a most inscrutable way.
A pinata of dreams
some split open like atoms,
others lapping like waves

in curvy ways
through time and space
far above my softening days
where laughter slides like window shades
and no one says BOO!

Words and Music

We've made it. We have rung out the old – the spending, the parties, the cheese balls, the ham … and rung in the new – a diet, a budget, hot soup and a fire. Who could ask for anything more?

Whether we ask them or not, the wordniks, that diverse but dedicated group intrigued by the English language, are taking the time to slide new words into our vocabulary and boot out a few of the old.

How many words do we have, anyway? More than we used to, for sure. Old English, the granddaddy of our language, ended up with a rousing 50,000: at the beginning Anglo Saxons only talked the talk, but by the 8th century they were writing words down. Think *Beowulf*.

Today's experts, after hedging, waffling, quantifying, and qualifying, estimate the English language weighs in at around a million words. An "educated person" knows about 20,000 of them, so it is said, and uses about 2,000 in a week … apparently not always in the best of spirits. Remember Eliza Doolittle's outburst? "Words, words, words, I'm so sick of words." Old or new, our fair lady is fed up.

Nevertheless, this time of the year words lovers flaunt their fads, favorites, fashions and feuds. For 2012 The *Merriam-Webster Dictionary* features 150 words so new they have yet to have a birthday; *Global Monitor*, a Texas word-tracking outfit has announced The Best Word, The Best Phrase and The Best Name of the year; and with mid-winter pizzazz, *The Dictionary of New Trendy Words* discloses some amazing new slang.

The Word of the Year for 2011, according Merriam-Webster – the word which was the most often looked up in their online dictionary

– is *Pragmatic* The publisher says searches for *pragmatic* jumped in the weeks before Congress voted last August to increase the nation's debt ceiling, and again as its 'super committee' tried to craft deficit-cutting measures in the fall.

One wonders about the winner for 2012? Which word, of the million we have to consider, will be looked up online most often? Unemployment? Default? Caucus? Chaos? Or will we lighten up? Do a search for "Eatie" perhaps. Eatie? The expression cooked up by in-the-kitchen expert Rachael Ray. No, not "foodie". We've been there, done that. Think *Eatie*. Oh, chocolates sweeter than wine.

"Never do I ever want to hear another word. There isn't one I haven't heard." Oh, yes there is. Eliza. I will spare you Merriam-Webster's entire list of new words, but here are a few: *Social media* and *tweet* made the cut, at last. Already confused? Think Facebook. Think Twitter. Moving on, a middle-aged woman seeking romance with a much younger man is now a *cougar* and a close, nonsexual friendship between two men, a *bromance. Helicopter parents?* Moms and dads who hover overhead, rarely out of reach, whether their children need them or not. A *boomerang child?* A young adult who moves back home for financial reasons. *M-commerce?* A new term for a business transaction conducted using a mobile electronic device such as a cell phone.

"I'm so sick of words!"

Robocall? A telephone call to a large number of people from an automated source that delivers a prerecorded message.

Me, too. Time to move on. In its twelfth annual survey of the English language around the world *Global Language Monitor,* a

Texas based outfit, announced their three top winners of 2011: *Occupy* was the Top Word, *Arab Spring* the Top Phrase and *Steve Jobs* the Top Name. (Jeopardy enthusiasts, take note.)

The Dictionary of Trendy Words has some cute slang. *Quarter pie* is fifteen minutes from now. Let's meet in a quarter pie! *Stiff* means being asleep. I was stiff for about 12 straight hours! *Jankway* is the trendy term for a wrong, long, or dangerous route to anywhere. I got lost and had to take the jankway. *Dip-Out?* To leave or go away. It's boring here! You want to dip-out and go to town? *Totally Salinda* means a lucid state of mind ... peace, love, and happiness ... hippy talk. This is the most beautiful day I've ever seen! Totally Salinda.

"Say one more word and I'll scream!"

"Shhh, here come the college kids from LSSU yanking words out of our language as fast as mouthful of bad teeth." For those who believe less is more, every New Year's Day since 1976 contrarian students from Michigan's Lake Superior State University (LSSU) banish words from "the Queen's English for Mis-Use, Over-Use and General Uselessness." They also give reasons why they don't want us to use them ever again.

Their most disdained word this year and why is *Amazing*: Hair is not amazing. Shoes are not amazing. My teeth grate, my hackles rise and even my dog is getting annoyed at this senseless overuse.. *Man Cave*: Not every man wants a recliner the size of a 1941 Packard that has a cooler in each arm and a holster for the remote. *Shared Sacrifice*: Usually used by politicians who wants other people to share in the sacrifice so they don't have to.

Occupy: The term Occupy Wall Street grew to become Occupy Anything You Want i.e. We are headed to Grandma's house – Occupy Thanksgiving is under way.

Pet Parents: Can a human being truly be a parent to a different species?

Baby Bump: It makes pregnancy sound like an in-style thing to do, not a serious choice.

Ginormous: No need to make a gigantic idiot out of yourself trying to find an enormous word for "big".

"Words, words, I get words all day through; Is that all you blighters can do?"

Blighters, eh?

I think she's got it.

Measuring Sticks

I am still much taller than The Little Girl
who once was me, bowl-shaped hair
and squinty eyes, posing on her birthday
in the sun in her favorite dress

with cherries down the front and no buttons
but shorter than the Mother I Once Was
tossing laughing babies lovingly,
knocking down cobwebs

crowning the tree with a star.
Shorter, surely, than the Matron I Became
ensconced in the rambler on the beach,
standing tall against a southern wind

hanging laundry high but feeling low
and down at least another half an inch
when I came to be the Divorced Old Lady
in the little condo on the hill

with the old stove and no ice, who was
asked to dog sit, for free. Why me?
You could use the company. You're all alone.
Where has everyone gone?

Clods of Thoughts

I wish I had inside shoes and outside shoes
Like some of my friends.
Coming or going? No problem.
They look at their feet.
Garden shoes (it's written on the bottom—Garden Shoes)
at the foot of the stairs, or in the back next to the hose.
Scuffs in the garage, flip flops beneath the bench on the porch
under the "Shoeless Joe Jackson is Welcome" sign.
Just joking ... about the sign, not the bench,
those unbending slats of clammy teak where guests
must strip to their toes.

How do some of my friends remember
which stay in and which stay out?
Mark them with felt pen?
The shoes, not the guests. They must.
Beige to match the carpet; blue like the sky.
Or does it take inside-outside minds to manage inside,
outside shoes? Inside, outside talk? Inside, outside friends?
An inside God, beige to match the carpet,
An outside God, blue like the sky.
Would that not be, to say the least, spiritually incorrect?
Apparently not, some of my friends use more shalts and shalt nots
than you can flick a twig at.

I've never seen some of my friends barefoot, inside or out.
Never have seen them hop—scattering clods of thoughts
like unworked soil in the spring
or splay pebbles into cracks of concrete with their toes.
They step out of their shoes as slick as flipping burgers
from a pan to a plate—left on the left, right on the right,

under the bench that is under the sign that says,
"Shoeless Joe Jackson is Welcome".
Just joking ... about the sign, not the friends.
... just some of my friends.
I have others.

Winner - 1st place, poetry, Portia Steele "Excellence in Poetry and Prose" contest, 2009

Who Says it First?

Goodbye ...
Not a satisfactory word
unless you're the one slamming the door
at best, the obligatory duet at the end of a chat
goodbye
goodbye
see ya
see ya
so much for that
movin' on

Some partings test time
like pistons out of synch
calls waiting
neighbors knocking
dogs barking
the buzzer, the beeper, the blink
gotta go
gotta pee
gotta gotta
bye bye.

Who says it first?
this means something.
soft thoughts blur like chiffon in the rain
secrets stutter
tears disappear
before they are able to drop
see ya
well ... bye

uh huh
oh shit
soft sigh

goodbye

Settling The Grounds

My grandmother did not have time for fortune tellers or believe in ESP, so I doubt if she would have tried to read tea leaves, even if she drank tea. Which she didn't. If my grandmother ever looked for answers at the bottom of her cup she was reading the coffee grounds. What else would you expect from a Scandinavian?

She used only one coffee pot that I remember: a large, smoky, aluminum affair, pock-marked from knocking around on the back of her wood and coal stove (itself a memory as black as a tin of shoe polish and as shiny as my grandfather's Sunday shoes). The handle, which basked all day in the heat without turning fiery hot, was dull and cracked, and the lid ended up so dented it didn't quite fit.

When my grandmother made coffee she filled the pot with cold water, dumped in a handful of grounds—regular grind, scooped out of a two pound can—threw in a pinch of salt, maneuvered a few more sticks of wood into the stove and went about her business … until the aroma of boiling coffee sent her running to the stove and pull yank pot off the heat just before it boiled over. With a sigh and a smile she grabbed a fistful of egg shells from a can on top of the stove and threw them in to the mix, not as an after thought but as a final touch. They bobbed around like marshmallows but eventually sank to the bottom, mottled and stained.

Egg shells were added to clarify the brew, my grandmother told me more as a matter of pride than an admission her coffee was so black and heavily boiled it needed clarification. Of course, she did not use the term "clarify". This was not the way she talked, wasting a three-syllable word for a simple task like making coffee.

She baked just as she brewed coffee: with an attitude. I watched that woman stick her entire arm inside the oven, hold it there until she counted to ten and determine if the temperature was suitable for cakes. Lined up on the dented silvery metal counter top in identical twin cake pans, the high round kind with a hole in the center, would be an angel food cake and a sponge cake. Never just one or the other. When I was little I thought sponge cake and angel food cake always came in pairs, like peanut butter and jelly or spaghetti and meatballs.

Not until years later did I realized this partnership was a marriage of convenience, based on the reality that my grandmother did not own a refrigerator. She would crack open a dozen eggs at a time, dump the yolks into the sponge cake batter, whip up the whites for angel food and throw the shells into the can on top of the stove. If she made just one cake what would she do with the other half of the eggs, keep them sitting around in her drippy little ice box? Not my grandmother.

She was not a woman to talk much. Perhaps years of hard work had turned her taciturn, but I think she was always more of a doer than a talker. She sprinkled her English with Swedish phrases such as uff da, words which she expelled with emotion, rather than a self-conscious intention to be bumper-sticker cute. Sometimes she fretted about the way she talked, as though she did not believe her English was as good as it should be after living in America for forty years; the way I remember it, people listened to her no matter what language she spoke.

Back to the coffee grounds. I hope grandma is having better luck these days, staring down into her big coffee cup in the sky. I said she might have read coffee grounds; I never said she read them well.

She promised me she would never leave her beach house, sitting over the waters of Liberty Bay in Puget Sound. She promised me, without my even thinking to ask, I could spend my summers there with her forever. And she made me promise never to dig for clams in the summertime (no matter that they were squirting up my pants legs, daring me to come and get them). I would drop dead, she said, on the spot if I ate so much as one clam in any month without an "r" in it.

She chastened me never to waste my time pulling up a horse clam. They're not much good for anything, and of course, I believed her. On her beach, over-populated as it was with butter clams, little necks, manillas and cockles, who needed horse clams anyway?

These days I stoop and grovel even for horse clams because there aren't many of the other kinds around, at least where I can dig. And these days I don't take the ferry to my grandmother's beach on Liberty Bay because grandma doesn't live there any more. My dad and my aunts sold the place to pay for her care after she had her leg amputated and grandma was so unhappy in the nursing home she died.

Where ever she is today I hope she has a rocky beach where all the clams are small and tender and that she has grown another leg the way the star fish do and that she is able to run across the kitchen again, and save the coffee just before it boils over.

My grandmother might have been wrong about some things but even when she was, she was a great teacher. She taught me a few words of Swedish, she taught me to love a wood fire, she taught me to start my day with the smells and the tastes of coffee. More important, it was from my grandmother I learned not to believe everything I hear, even when folks throw in a few egg shells just to clarify the matter.

Quantum Leap

Time clutches the walls of our minds
like chattering leaves.
time on my hands
time marches on
time is money
my time or your time
long time no see
he's doin' time.
It's all about time.
Hard time.
Big time.
Time marches on.

The significance of a single moment is as difficult to grab as a
snowflake.
Between the aim and the fire,
a tick and a tock,
the I and the do,
the pitch, and the hit, and the woo,
a heart can sputter and start.
A plane may waver.
A dozing soul might awaken.

A moment is a bead before it dangles on a string,
a grain of sand before it joins the beach,
a star without a galaxy,
a note without a symphony,
the pause between the letters that makes words.

Moments fill the gaps between the particles which shape the earth,
the stars, the universe, the sky, the sea, the trees,

the island where no man is unto himself
(although we think we are alone, without a trace of place)
straining, through the fog, listening for the blip out in the mist.
It is a moment.
Grab it.

Summer's End

A wilted rose reclined in a press,
wing nuts cinched just enough to shrivel her,
petal by petal
from the outside in,
is a queen in a sarcophagus
compared to me, a butcher
wrapping the bloody remains of each day
in paper or plastic
and string,
yearning to sprawl among pillows
and cower under down,
while slits of soft space
let my dreams slip out and in
like pumpkins on the town.

Melt Down

across the street in the vacant lot
(we call it the green belt)
a cluster of unbending firs starts to quiver.
Old snow
Tired snow
no place to go but down snow.
unruly branches of ice
break on our heads, shiver our spines
and hit the ground in crunchy thuds
like toddlers sprawled on the floor
in the grocery store
The party's over.

The Age of Sweet Rebellion

Where I come from we grow an onion we call the Walla Walla Sweet. It takes only one summer for a Walla Walla Sweet to prove it is fine to be both sugary and sharp. It took me years to realize what is true for an onion is also true for me.

I want to bite like an onion resting on a slice of soft, white bread. I want to ooze like a chocolate-covered cherry just before it explodes in my mouth. I want to wear the label of the mustards that I love — hot and spicy, sweet and smooth. I want to listen to a bold, brassy trumpet battle with a mellow alto sax. I want to float like a butterfly, sting like a bee. What's good enough for Muhammad Ali is good enough for me.

If I end up sliced on a slab I want to be viewed as marble cake: swirled with sweet musky vanilla and bittersweet chocolate; flavored with honey and vinegar; entwined with rosebuds; embellished with thorns.

I was taught the sweet part early on. When I was young I gobbled up only the vanilla and the honey and the rosebuds. I wanted as much sweetness as I could shovel in since I figured the whole point of living is to be nice.

My mother said, "You are mommy's nice little girl." My grandmother scowled, "Now you be nice, young lady." On my report card teachers wrote She is a good student and nice to her classmates, She is a sweet little girl, My, she has lovely manners. It is not surprising when I grew up I wanted to be – a nice woman.

Nobody warned me that sweetness without a sting is trampled like a garden without a fence, killed like a cat without claws, shriveled like a child without love.

It took more than a decade before I vowed to shed my "nice" reputation if it killed me. And it almost did. I decided to start smoking, with the help of two highly regarded institutions: the tobacco industry and the University of Washington.

Once a week, at lunch time in the campus cafeteria, clean cut men dressed in blazers and sharply creased slacks, and perky women with bouncy hair and glistening lips stood on the stairway and showered us with sample packs of cigarettes. Students, from entering freshmen like me to worldly upperclassmen, scrambled for them just as children scoop up candy tossed by clowns.

Everyone lit up except for me. I stashed my booty until I could practice alone. A nice young woman doesn't want an audience as she teeters on the brink of sophistication.

I took the step on a rainy, late autumn afternoon. I remember I wore a yellow slicker. I kept thrusting my hand into one of the big patch pockets stroking the smooth unopened cellophane wrappers of my practice cigarettes. My purpose, as I marched up the broad gray stairs of the Seattle Public Library, was twofold – research and smoking.

I smoked in the cold, chipped tile bathroom in the basement. These days I hear that perverts haunt public restrooms, but the only company I had were gurgling toilets and faucets dripping rust. First I smoked and then climbed upstairs to take notes and downstairs to smoke and up and down and up and down. It took a half a dozen trips to the library before my paper was finished; by that time I could inhale with a steady stomach and blow smoke out my nose. By the time the grades came out I was addicted.

Thirty years later I quit. People were referring to me as that nice woman ... with the bad cough. I got rid of it, but at the same time I didn't feel nice anymore. My children drove me crazy. My neighbors were boring. The mailman was a jerk and the dog was stupid. I was a hypocrite, a fake, a fraud, play-acting, role-playing.

If I wasn't nice anymore, what was I? I wasn't anything at all.

What I needed, although I didn't know it at the time, was to be like an onion. I still wanted to be sweet – to ooze like a chocolate covered cherry just before it explodes in my mouth – but I also wanted to bite like a slab of onion poised on a slice of soft, white bread. I wanted to be the brazen trumpet who gets to out-blare the mellow alto sax. I wanted to float like a butterfly, sting like a bee. What was good enough for Muhammad Ali was good enough for me.

I dreamt about antonyms of nice: awful, dreadful, disagreeable; unfriendly, ill-bred; sloppy, careless and crude. How cool. How honest.

It is as ridiculous to act nice when I am miserable, or be sweet when I am furious, or go along with the group just because I don't want to be unpleasant as it is for a Walla Walla Sweet to hide under a crust and try to pass as dessert. I might not be the sharpest knife in the drawer, but at the moment it is enough to be simply a woman without a cough who savors the bite of an onion.

Windfall

An inadvertent happiness is moving in.
it comes upon me unexpectedly
like an askant font
punctuating a page of Helvetica prose.

A jolt while I plod in the dark to the john,
a sun bolt as I tumble the dryer
no need to hang out
even if I had the lines and inclination.

An "aha" halts my gridlock reverie
with a distillation of the moment,
pure as scotch whisky
a jaw-dropping blast of ... what else but happiness?

It floods me for no reason when I am alone,
No regard for my supply or demand.
No way to share it.
It is a windfall, like apples, no questions asked.

Donkey Kong

He pins the three monkeys of no evil on my backside
See no... hear no... speak no...
I don't.
He kicks me.
I won't.
He kicks me again
then freezes me with his smile.
White hot smoke rings blow through his teeth
licking my rear.
A Cheshire cat who won't disappear.
Kick me.
Lick me.
Kick me, again.

Mark My Words

If our world is to end up balanced
nothing awry
not in our world
not at the end, anyway, then
when you start talking religion... again
don't ask me if I believe in God, because
instead of getting an answer
I'll give you a question.

How are you defining God these days, eh?
This will ultimately upset the fine balance between
the ask and the you shall receive marks of punctuation.
Let us pretend I simply say agree
there is such a one in whom I believe,
You will assume my God is your God
(there is only one, eh)
He is in both of our heavens
all's right with the world.
Amen.

Or She?

I am apt to answer a question with a question
even though I know that one last answer,
like the cheese,
will stand alone at the end, and
The Second Coming will begin with a question.
It won't be my fault
will it?

Home Schooled

My baby loves a blue-gray box
three inches by two inches by one, and
my baby loves his shiny, purple peg.
He puffs and shakes and slobbers bubbles
down his chin until the lid popped off;
with a grunt he wiggles in the peg
(it has to be the purple one)
and pats down the lid
with a questionable sigh
like setting in a jigsaw piece.

My baby crouches
like a cat with an eye in a mouse hole.
Quiver and sit.
Tremble and wait.
The quietest time of my every day
until he explodes, rises on his toes,
shaking the box with a passion, and
finally flings off the lid in a frenzy.
He sidle-eyes me with a chuckle.
His peg is always there
still shiny
still purple

still in the box.
He sidle-eyes me with a nod and a chuckle.
We are learning trust.

There is More than Pie in the Sky

I look up a lot, these days, the way kids do, or down to watch ants or straight into the distance at sunsets dripping over our mountains like syrup on ice cream.

In the northwest corner of Washington state where I live, on the fourth of July, Independence Day, we watch as rockets and roman candles light up the night sky. We have good reason not to look up the rest of the year: mountains left and right meet us eye to eye; Puget Sound laps against the western horizon; rivers rush, streams meander, and shimmering lakes await us. Looking up generally gets us a face full of rain for no reason.

But there are times … at least there once was a time … it was March, not July … when I begrudgingly flicked a glance towards the heavens. I had dozens of things yet to do, "miles to go" as they say, but everyone else was standing around outside with chins pointed skyward.

The parting of clouds should be reason enough to make me look up and enjoy. Evening sky in the northwest in March is not usually as streaked with color as it was that night, as cloud pillows contained in pastel cases scurried overhead while black shadows lurked just above the horizon, ready to pounce. If that was all there was in the sky that evening – the parting of clouds – I would have missed it.

The coming forth of stars should be reason enough to make me look up and enjoy. I once wondered about stars, how they move around in the sky but somehow stay connected. When I remember to look I can still spot Orion, ready to shoot, the Seven Sisters huddled together, and the two dippers hanging on their celestial pegs. But most of the time I forget that they are staring down at me.

If that was all there was in the sky that evening – the parting of clouds and the coming forth of stars – I would have missed it.

The presence of the moon should be reason enough to make me look up and enjoy, especially when it is as full as a sunflower in August. But, when you've seen one full moon you've seen them all, that's how I had been figuring. A peripheral glance as I take out the garbage is plenty moon for me. If that was all there was in the sky that evening – the parting of clouds and the coming forth of stars and a huge cheddar moon – I would have missed it.

The sight of a shadow nibbling away at the moon should be reason enough to make me look up and enjoy. I figured a glance will suffice. No need to get hysterical the way they did in the old days. They didn't know an eclipse of the moon is merely Earth throwing its shadow around, the way children cast floppy-eared shadows on the opposite wall with their fingers. If that was all there was in the sky that evening – the parting of clouds and the coming forth of stars and the crumbling away of the moon – I would have missed it.

A vision of a visitor among the stars should be reason enough to make me look up and enjoy. I had planned to do just that, but the night was cold and the wind kicked up; a glimpse of a comet out my front window was all I had time and energy for. I didn't take my binoculars out of the drawer. If that was all there was in the sky that evening – first the parting of clouds, next the coming forth of stars, then a big round yellow moon turning black, and finally a the sight of a comet passing by – I would have missed it.

But everything showed up at once. The clouds, the stars, the moon, the comet … and me. Actually, it was the clamor of barefoot children I have never heard before and grownups I had never seen before, in their slippers, that drew me outside.

From my back yard I saw clouds pulling back like curtains drawn for a play and I watched the moon shrink like Alice did when she fell into wonderland. The darker the sky became the shinier grew the stars. At the same time, as I trotted around to the front, I followed the path of a comet streaking across the sky.

I couldn't stand still. I paced from front yard to back to front to back until the moon took pity on me and rose high enough so that I could stand in one place and see the whole thing: a comet with a forked tail blazing a trail over a darkening, star-cluttered sky, while a black rubber stamped moon dimmed the clouds.

This was not a play, it was a four ring circus and to think, if I had waited until the fourth of July to look up I would have missed the whole thing.

Refolding a Swan

When a stately paper swan
creased into crisp existence
by steadfast fingers,
(no dots to draw to
no B for every A
no pencil, no ruler, no glue)
comes undone
he is never the same.
Never again so pristine
never so treasured, never so dear.

Just one more used bird.
No reason for being.
Recycled on Monday morning
along with the string of dolls
from yesterday's news.
Accordion pleated we called it
then cut into lives
by sweaty dented fingers
clutching dull pointy scissors for kids.
With a quick flick of a tiny wrist

Voila, there they are
a band of sisters,
holding hands,
skirts judiciously joined
with half a child clinging at the end
like half a life left over.
I always wanted to snip her off
but I never did.

I loved her like all the rest...
but not as much.

Winner - 1st place, "Everyday Musing" contest, sponsored by ReadMe Publishing, 2009

The Buzz

Be sad for crones with fingers heavy
with twinkly diamonds on wrinkly skin
and crimson badges of battle
perched on blue-moussed coiffures
slightly askew, like their smiles.

Stand back from women with outlined lips
shades carefully match their hats
with no intention to stay in the lines,
like captive daffodils
stuffed in jars of green water.

Stay clear of clubbers clicking their pumps
like metronomes running amok
whose shiny, sausage-like, matronly legs,
sashay to a saintly beat.
Busy, busy, busy, very busy.

Pri Tee Good

How ya doing?
Pri tee good.
What a lie.
Don't they know?

How ya doing?
Oh, pri tee good.
Am I shy or playing lets pretend?
Don't they care?

How ya doing?
The usual.
Pri tee good is a sacrifice fly,
a pretty good way to move on
to important stuff like the weather.

Snapshot in Sepia

I remember that day

It was August …
I'm standing tall
in my soft washed blue pinafore
cherries polka-dotting down the front.
the fifteenth …
my lips pressed like a dour old lady
but a tug of a smile inside
where no one can see it.
I was five now …
sweaty hands dangling like mittens on a string
slitted eyes underlining serious bangs
face sunblasted
two bees buzzing my neck.
floppy roses climbing up my back
I want my lemonade and cake right now.
everybody's laughing at me.
I don't want a scrapbook
stand still and don't talk and say cheese.
What's a scrapbook for?

Where's the rest of the people?
They must all be dead by now.
Then, Mom, then! Where is the rest of the roll?
Oh, I don't know.
That was a long time ago.

The Count Down

Twenty four of us ended up on the left of the center aisle, four to a bench, not alphabetically but according to some prearranged plan of the court.

Shortly after eight in the morning we had wandered in one by one and spread out on either side of the courtroom. I grabbed an aisle spot and settled in, not sure what would come next. After the suits and the robe filed in the judge slowly called out our names as we gathered our belongings and slid into our assigned seats as quietly as books on a shelf.

My seat was in the third row from the front next to a pert woman in a becoming maroon woolen coat and flowing scarf, soon loosened and untied. On my right was a comfortable looking young fellow - brush hair cut, jeans, casual brown cotton sweater. A gaunt man barely balancing on the edge of middle age perched on the aisle seat in front of me. In his white shirt, stripped tie and tan checkered jacket he was thin beyond belief.

Some of our group swiveled around, smiling, waving and shaking their heads slightly as though to say what are you doing here or how is it that we have ended up together, out of context? I envied them their comfort in finding a familiar face.

Next came introductions: the judge in his robes; the two attorneys (defense, older in a navy blue suit; prosecutor, taller wearing muted grayish brown). They started right in asking us questions, not as many as I expected and not very telling to my inexperienced ear.

They acted like as though knew us, probably from the information we mailed in weeks before. Each of us was encouraged to speak at least once; a few talked quite a lot while others, like me, had to be encouraged with direct questions. The attorney in gray wondered if I thought a breathalyzer test was unfair, considering not everyone reacts to alcohol the same way. I rambled something about it was probably the best we could do, just as we all have the same speed limits although some of us drive better than others. It is no wonder my mindset was more on driving than drinking. I had just traveled rather briskly over fifty odd miles in the darkness of early morning on unfamiliar roads with more curves than a bag of pretzels to get to the courthouse on time.

Far sooner than I expected we were rustled out of the courtroom. "Remember your seats," chastened the judge. Just time to use the bathrooms, unkink our legs, inhale a few breaths of fresh air before we were called back.

Without preamble the judge read six of our names and thanked and excused the remainder. He spoke so quickly and quietly I wasn't sure what he said, except for one name. My name. No doubt about it, I had become one-sixth of a jury.

The frail man was not, the perky woman was not. I did not even notice their leaving. I focused on the five who remained. The young man next to me was still there. Even though we did nothing but nod he was the closest thing to a friend I had in the room. Directly in front of me was a quiet woman, a shiny gray pony tail trailing down to her waist, clutching a yellow paperback book of puzzles under her arm. Earlier, as she took off her coat I had noticed her dark gray shirt was on backwards. Later on in the day she had turned it around.

The other jurors were behind me: an imposing, older man in a roomy white pullover; a short, ruddy faced, stiff-mouthed man wearing a plaid shirt; an affable woman who belonged to the voice I had been hearing behind me. I don't know what they thought about me. We were strangers in an unfamiliar place with an uncertain day ahead. That's all that I knew.

The jury room was quiet as we waited to be called. Sitting around the table just the right size for six we were comfortable enough, but silent. Plenty to think about. No reason to share. I can't believe I'm here. That's what I was thinking.

When we were summoned into the courtroom everyone was standing and we all sat down together; "everyone" being the judge, the two attorneys and the defendant, a smallish man in a dark red corduroy shirt. I could see only the right side of his face as he sat stone like, staring straight ahead.

Our work as jurors was taxing but not arduous; early on we were given a break while discussions went on in the courtroom. Our little room already felt like home, a quiet place to reconnect fleeting impressions: the judge, immutable eyes behind dignified glasses; the prosecutor, the more restrained of the two; the defense attorney, more bustling; the defendant, as still as the air around him.

Next, testimony from two sheriffs, a state trooper and a toxicologist. Then out for a lunch break as the six of us went our separate ways. I found a Thai place nearby with a table for one and a newspaper. Under these circumstances it was easy to follow the firm instructions of the judge - do not discuss the case, not with each other, not with anyone.

That's one plus for our jury. We did not open up to each other: not one word, not a shrug or a frown or a smile. As we sat in our room (not locked in it was made clear, the rest of the world was locked out) not once did we make anything but the smallest of talk. Not once did anyone allude to the fact there was no majority rules option for us; to reach a verdict we had to agree.

As the rain clouds darkened and the clock ticked through the afternoon it became clear we would be back the next day. Witnesses kept coming, friends and coworkers of the defendant. Pieces of evidence: photographs, a meal and drink tab; a breathalyzer test. Testimony: how acetones and hydrocarbons can effect the results of the breathalyzer; police reports; medical reports; test results. At the end of the day I finally saw the defendant full faced as he took the stand, looked straight ahead and told his story.

Decision making time came the next day, late in the morning. I knew my inclination but I had no expectations about the rest of the jury. I has been so preoccupied with the trial itself I hadn't given the finale much thought. I would have imagined impassioned conversation, perhaps three of us on one side of the table and three on the other pulling strings, twisting, tying knots. All of us talking by turns, all of us listening to each other as intently as we had listened in the courtroom. But when push came to shove, as the saying goes, I would have envisioned the blacks and whites of our six separate existences weaving together into a fabric we would unroll before the court in a measured but timely manner. We all had places to go and things to do.

I would have expected some of us to talk more, others to listen more. Some to give. Some to take. At worst I would have expected we would quickly run the gamut of dribbles and double talk and nuances and fine points and what is reasonable and what is doubt and all the other posturing and histrionics which are part of talking things through. But I would have assumed, static or not, our antennas would pick up the same station.

A scant ten minutes later I watched ten eyes turn to me for acquiescence. Then five fingers pointed at me and three chairs pulled back from the table. The man in the plaid shirt, the same man who had chatted to me about his farm, his native country, his sons leaned forward and shot in my face some of the most vitriolic words which had ever come my way. Then he said he had enough of me, turned around and faced the wall.

At that moment the sandwiches came and that was how we ate lunch. I stared straight ahead, nibbled at my tuna fish sandwich until I noticed I was not able to swallow, wrapped it up and stuck it in my purse. One way or another I knew I would be going home soon and it might be a long, lonely ride. The choice was mine.
By that time would I be the bimbo as dense as a black hole, the broad who couldn't tell Truth from a hole in the ground, the one out of six who dug herself a hole with her doubt and then jumped in with both feet?

Or would I drive home in glory. All I would have to do is agree. Maybe he is guilty. After all, isn't it a judgment call, like how high is an infield fly or whether the ball carrier stepped over the line? My jury would be so happy with me. We would exchange email addresses and phone numbers and plan to have lunch together some day. Not that it would ever happen, but I wanted to be included in the fantasy. But first would come the drive home and if I didn't like the company I didn't want to go.

The puzzle woman found a pencil. The chatty woman spoke loudly and fast, as though she were a misbegotten hostess of an ill-conceived dinner party. The man in the plaid shirt stood and chewed. I could see his ears moving. "You are going to have to stand out there in front of everybody and say not guilty when the rest of us say guilty," he finally spit out. "They're going to ask us all, you know. They're going to know you are the one."

I looked at the young man, our foreman, and told him I had a question for judge. He leaped up with a pencil and pad, trying his best to make us all come out even. The way to ask a question when the world is locked out is to summon a messenger by phone, hand her the folded paper, and wait for an answer from the judge. Twice I sent questions. Twice came replies. Both answers exacerbated my doubt, which is strange, because these same comments confirmed the verdict of guilt which lay like concrete in the five minds of my peers.

They said I did not ask the right questions. If you don't like my questions ask your own questions, I retorted. The same words which were pleasantries in earlier hours were not working for us now. It was five against one. I knew I could never change all of their minds. Not if we never got home. Easier for them to change mine. Quick and easy. Who's to know?

I nodded to the young man and he knew it was time to pick up the phone. We single filed into the courtroom and stood while our foreman read the verdict. Nobody polled the jury. Nobody said anything. All we had to do was walk out single file leaving behind one judge, two attorneys and one defendant, still wearing his red corduroy shirt.

The lobby was quiet, the parking lot motionless but in the distance trees bent in the wind. I walked quickly without turning to saying goodbye, not that there was anyone who wanted to hear another word from me.

I drove easily. It was stormy but still daylight and the stretch of windy roads was familiar. By the time I got home my eyes were dry and my tuna sandwich was still on the seat beside me looking as limp as I felt. Limp without joy but limp without guilt. There is only the trip. One mile after another.

While Reading Haruki Murakami

Kafka's at the bottom of the well
not a misstep
he climbed back down
but he can't find his chair
bemused, he hums
The ladder's still standing, baby
bring down the extra stool blues.

82

Careless Love

I never heard music until I found jazz
really heard it
felt it
loved it as though it were mine
Before jazz ...
what with working all night and schooling all day...
I had no music.
I was a zombie, a fool
Hey, I couldn't carry a tune.
I didn't play anything but the radio
Still can't. Still don't
Can't even clap right (so my ex-husband said)
No one to talk to.
All by myself

Maybe I didn't find jazz, after all
more than likely, it was jazz that found me
When you're marching and you're happy, clap your hands
That's jazz
When you're dragging and you're bluesy, all alone
That's jazz
When you're great and when you know it
When you're beat and really show it
When you're quiet and tippy toe it
That's jazz

Who could have known
jazz would literally be blown out of town?
No street to strut down, no place to play
We couldn't find jazz to save our souls

but jazz found us in a heartbeat.
As long as we laugh, there is jazz
As long as we cry, there is jazz
Love, oh love, oh careless love

Four Seventeen Syllable Stories

A voting booth for
two, eye to eye, you and the
not so you. Who blinks?

Left turns, right turns meet
in time-space past direction.
Which is the right path?

Concentration rules.
Where oh where went the moment?
Well, maybe next year.

Always be mindful
but never watch yourself think.
Throw away mirrors.

My Spirit is a Yo-Yo

I am earthbound, my feet glued to the ground and my body, attached to my feet. I have no truck with previous lives or prophesies, and that old black magic casts no shadow on me.

My spirit (or soul or whatever you want to call that thing everyone has hidden deep inside) is a yo-yo. I can sleep it or walk the dog with it or play round the world with it, but it is always tethered. It might wander a bit, but it never goes far off the track.

I am what you see; my spirit is what you get; the two of us are grounded to the max. Our place is here; our time is now. We don't believe in UFO's, or ESP, and when it comes to Out of Body Experiences, we pass.

I'm not claiming these things don't happen; they just never happen to me. If a flying saucer should touch down in my neighborhood I wouldn't hesitate to stick around and chat with the crew. If the little green men offered me a ride through time and space I would go and take notes and sell them to the tabloids, but nothing so exotic ever happens to me.

I swear, if I died and came back to life I would not be able to relate even one near death experience I could turn into a book to flaunt on all the talk shows. No bright light. No aura. No peace. Nothing. If my body ever goes through one of these experiences I know I will sleep right through it and wake up on the other side—of the bed.

When I was ten my grandmother from Minnesota gave me a Ouija board. She wasn't a witch or anything like that, she was an old Norwegian woman who wore her long gray hair in a bun. She bought my board in the toy department at the five-and-dime and had no idea some spoil sports think the game is an instrument of the devil. The whole point of the Ouija experience is to place a round disk called a planchette on a board decorated with the alphabet, numbers, stars and moons. You get yourself a partner and both of you lightly set your fingers on the disk and ask it questions.

That round piece of wood would skate all over the board spelling out phrases, pointing to numbers, sometimes sashaying straight toward Yes and then making a U-turn toward No. Nobody, not even me and certainly not my cousins, would admit we were purposely pushing the little planchette. We didn't even realize it. Eventually I was the one who owned up that I thought the game was a self-inflicted hoax. Even when I was a kid my spirit was hog-tied to my brain.

When I heard about research on psychic phenomena done at the University of Chicago I paid attention. Researchers at this prestigious institution took a survey which revealed that 175 million adults in the United States have had mystical, religious experiences. The experts comment, "A person who has it (a religious or mystical experience) is religious whether he goes to church or not, whether he professes any doctrine or not, simply because he claims to have seen and to know the way things really are."

The way things really are? How could 175 million Americans know the way things really are when nothing stays the same? Hemlines rise and fall like window shades. Light shifts back and forth from particles to waves. The universe keeps on expanding and space has started to curve. It only goes to prove that 175 million Americans can be wrong.

I asked a five year old if he knew the difference between real and make-believe. "Sure," he said without even stopping to think. "Sometimes things that used to be make-believe turn into real."

"Like what," I asked.

"Like walking on the moon. That used to be make-believe and now it is real."

I didn't know what to make of this kid. Is he like us, my spirit and me, down-to-earth, matter-of-fact and practical or is he from the other side, peeking over the edge?

My spirit and I find enough kicks to keep us going right here on earth. Like in April when that extra hour floats in the window like Cinderella home from the ball. Are those sixty extra minutes real or are they make-believe? Where did they comes from? Where are they going? Is it as risky to push around the hands of a clock as it is to force a Ouija board to give answers?

We don't have all the answers, my spirit and I. All we know is that our place is here, our life is short and we have miles to go. So, when it comes to UFO's or ESP or Out of Body Experiences, we'll pass. The same goes for astral travel. We just don't have the time.

Scherenschnitte

I am paper
He is scissors
Scissors cuts paper

I am paper
He is rock
Paper covers rock

Clunk
Rock covers paper
I am paper

Who will play his game when I die
Then who will he cover and cut?
He might go first

I could write my own verse.
If Popeye can say I yam what I yam
Why then oh why can not I?

Sunday Drive

I present to him the children
elbows, ears, fingernails, toes
pristine as four chubby male bodies can be,
who sternly marches them to the car.
slam, bang
honk, honk

Bigheaded with rollers, half out of my robe
I tap on the window
tumbling hair filtering his Sunday smirk.
I'm coming! I'm coming! I mouthed with a shout.
honkety honk

Alone, no longer behind before I begin
overly ready, quiveringly ready
a sweaty earring denting my hands
a frozen honk stuck to my gut
just yesterday's chopped liver.

Score

Death is not remembering you've ever
been alive? I read that some place,
twice. Strange how a figure of speech
has a life of its own

Life is not remembering you've ever
been dead? Doesn't work ... or does it?
Must a metaphor be as structured as a steeple?
you never see one pointed down

You have to live until the end
or the ripple you are making
doesn't have a finish
and the finish in life is as important

As that last burst of speed
when the silken streak gets behind the crease
and fires the ball over the goalie's shoulder
not nil to nil any more.

Scattered Thoughts

Bits and pieces cling to my brain
like crumbs on a cupcake wrap
hide in my soul, eat at my heart
dart to wherever it is lost thoughts go

I can never say quite as much as I know
never recall all of a dream
never stick in my thumb and pull out a whole plum
or reveal quite as much as I feel

Thoughts ooze through my brain like candle wax,
drip to another's mind, stick to another page
where I read them and scream
why didn't I think of that?

Salt Is More Than a Seasoning

I was born between mountains and water and so far I have found no reason to leave. In the morning I watch mountains strung along the eastern sky like paper dolls snipped from sheets of white. If I follow the sun I end the day gazing at another set of peaks, smaller perhaps and more distant, but blazing with color– red, orange and yellow spread across the sky like wildfires.

Even so, I could live without mountains if I had to; it is Puget Sound I cannot do without. I can't imagine what it would be like to live far away from waters that are always on the prowl: home for gulls and ferry boats and pilings fringed with barnacles; edged with smooth flat rocks meant for skipping; fringed with beaches; frosted with foam.

I need to sail pebbles sidearm every now and then, trying to get them to hop across the waves at least three times. I need to meet up with a gust of wind that has a little spunk, that dares deposit smells of salt and seaweed and touches of sand on my skin and in my hair and up my nose.

Puget Sound is my special delight and my special memory. I remember bouncing under an abandoned dock with my grandmother in her round bottom boat built by an old Swede who lived up the beach. As we embarked she lurched herself upright and then half fell between the oars with the help of a long-handled tool concocted by my grandfather: an ugly C-shaped black rod pointed at one end, lashed to a pole the size of a broomstick. My grandmother would never get in the boat without it.

Under the dock, even on a hot August day, it was dark and cool and creepy. The shadows were brownish like an old sepia portrait.

Balancing herself in the boat, lit up in mustard strips of sunlight, stood a woman already almost old, flailing at the pilings and not paying any attention to the child huddled on a wooden seat, a little bit scared but already so in love with Puget Sound she would never ask to be rowed back to shore. When the rusty coffee can was full of pile worms we went trolling, for anything but dogfish.

Puget Sound is an arm of the Pacific Ocean, a tentacle so to speak, that stretches around mountains and fingers its way through valleys, never far away but capable of playing hide and seek. Sometimes, as we come to the top of a hill there it is lying there, just below us, or way ahead in the distance, or a little to the left, always a surprise, sometimes sparkling with waves and sprinkled with sailboats.

We breathe in the smells of salty water without even trying and often without noticing until an incoming tide and a strong breeze delivers us a whiff of air so salty we remember we are alive. It is the same feeling as when we lie around and watch football the entire Thanksgiving Day and don't even notice the odors creeping out of the oven until we go out for an arm load of firewood and scurry back inside. We get blasted with the smell of sizzling turkey. That's what it is like for me when I go away and then come home to Puget Sound.

I like our mountains but I don't love them. I don't know why.

Perhaps they're too standoffish. There are times when I marvel at the morning sun peering out from behind a peak like a child looking through the rungs of a crib. And I gape just like everyone when a glowing snow-capped peak emerges through the clouds. The beauty of mountains in the sunshine is our pay back for putting up with all the rain. Although I admire the grandeur of our mountains they are too aloof for me to love.

Puget Sound is family. I dunk my fingers in it and splash in it and taste it and float on it and dig around the edges. It gets in my lungs and clings to my hair. I always have. I always will. It suits me.